CW01590596

Date:

Message:

Words of Hope™

Footprints

christian art gifts®

Footprints

First edition 2016

Designed by Christian Art Gifts

Images used under license from Shutterstock.com

Printed in China

ISBN 978-1-4321-1615-6

16 17 18 19 20 21 22 23 24 25 – 10 9 8 7 6 5 4 3 2 1

FOOTPRINTS

One night I had a dream.
I was walking along the beach with the Lord,
and across the skies flashed scenes of my life.
In each scene I noticed two sets of footprints in the sand.
One was mine, and one was the Lord's.
When the last scene of my life appeared before me,
I looked back at the footprints in the sand,
and to my surprise I noticed that many
times along the path of my life
there was only one set of footprints,
and I noticed that it was at the lowest and
saddest times in my life.
I asked the Lord about it:
"Lord, You said that once I decided to follow You,
You would walk with me all the way.
But I notice that during the most troublesome times
in my life there is only one set of footprints.
I don't understand why You left my side
when I needed You most."
The Lord said: "My precious child, I never
left you during your time of trial.
Where you see only one set of footprints,
it was then that I carried you."

Contents

Our Dream –
God's Plan

OUR DREAM – GOD'S PLAN

"I know the plans I have for you," says the LORD. "They are plans for good and not for disaster, to give you a future and a hope."

Jeremiah 29:11 NLT

Many are the plans in a person's heart, but it is the LORD's purpose that prevails.

Proverbs 19:21 NIV

The counsel of the LORD stands forever, the plans of His heart to all generations.

Psalm 33:11 ESV

The LORD has made everything for His own purposes, even the wicked for a day of disaster.

Proverbs 16:4 NLT

The LORD Almighty has sworn, "Surely, as I have planned, so it will be, and as I have purposed, so it will happen."

Isaiah 14:24 NIV

The LORD has told you what is good, and this is what He requires of you: to do what is right, to love mercy, and to walk humbly with your God.

Micah 6:8 NLT

You saw me before I was born. Every day of my life was recorded in Your book. Every moment was laid out before a single day had passed. How precious are Your thoughts about me, O God. They cannot be numbered!

Psalm 139:16-17 NLT

OUR DREAM – GOD'S PLAN

Commit to the LORD whatever you do, and He will establish your plans.

Proverbs 16:3 NIV

Hope deferred makes the heart sick, but a dream fulfilled is a tree of life.

Proverbs 13:12 NLT

Delight yourself in the LORD, and He will give you the desires of your heart.

Psalm 37:4 ESV

We are God's masterpiece. He has created us anew in Christ Jesus, so we can do the good things He planned for us long ago.

Ephesians 2:10 NLT

You made all the delicate, inner parts of my body and knit me together in my mother's womb. Thank You for making me so wonderfully complex! Your workmanship is marvelous – how well I know it.

Psalm 139:13-14 NLT

The word of the LORD came to me, saying, "Before I formed you in the womb I knew you, and before you were born I consecrated you; I appointed you a prophet to the nations."

Jeremiah 1:4-5 ESV

God created mankind in His own image, in the image of God He created them; male and female He created them.

Genesis 1:27 NIV

"Everyone who is called by My name, whom I have created for My glory; I have formed him, yes, I have made him."

Isaiah 43:7 NKJV

Serve the LORD with gladness! Come into His presence with singing! Know that the LORD, He is God! It is He who made us, and we are His; we are His people, and the sheep of His pasture.

Psalm 100:2-3 ESV

The LORD God formed man of the dust of the ground, and breathed into his nostrils the breath of life; and man became a living being.

Genesis 2:7 NKJV

Even before He made the world, God loved us and chose us in Christ to be holy and without fault in His eyes. God decided in advance to adopt us into His own family by bringing us to Himself through Jesus Christ.

Ephesians 1:4-5 NLT

The Spirit of God has made me; the breath of the Almighty gives me life.

Job 33:4 NIV

"Are not two sparrows sold for a copper coin? And not one of them falls to the ground apart from your Father's will. But the very hairs of your head are all numbered. Do not fear therefore; you are of more value than many sparrows."

Matthew 10:29-31 NKJV

"You didn't choose Me. I chose you. I appointed you to go and produce lasting fruit, so that the Father will give you whatever you ask for, using My name."

John 15:16 NLT

In Him also we have obtained an inheritance, being predestined according to the purpose of Him who works all things according to the counsel of His will, that we who first trusted in Christ should be to the praise of His glory.

Ephesians 1:11-12 NKJV

What is man that You are mindful of him, and the son of man that You care for him? Yet You have made him a little lower than the heavenly beings and crowned him with glory and honor.

Psalm 8:4-5 ESV

God Guides

GOD GUIDES

The LORD will guide you always; He will satisfy your needs in a sun-scorched land and will strengthen your frame. You will be like a well-watered garden, like a spring whose waters never fail.

Isaiah 58:11 NIV

Jesus said to him, "I am the way, the truth, and the life. No one comes to the Father except through Me."

John 14:6 NKJV

Show me Your ways, LORD, teach me Your paths. Guide me in Your truth and teach me, for You are God my Savior, and my hope is in You all day long.

Psalm 25:4-5 NIV

GOD GUIDES

Send out Your light and Your truth; let them guide me. Let them lead me to Your holy mountain, to the place where You live.

Psalm 43:3 NLT

Thus says the LORD who made it, the LORD who formed it to establish it: "Call to Me, and I will answer you, and show you great and mighty things, which you do not know."

Jeremiah 33:2-3 NKJV

Your word is a lamp to guide my feet and a light for my path.

Psalm 119:105 NLT

Teach me to do Your will, for You are my God! Let Your good Spirit lead me on level ground!

Psalm 143:10 ESV

May the Lord direct your hearts into God's love and Christ's perseverance.

2 Thessalonians 3:5 NIV

The LORD directs the steps of the godly. He delights in every detail of their lives. Though they stumble, they will never fall, for the LORD holds them by the hand.

Psalm 37:23-24 NLT

He guides the humble in what is right and teaches them His way.

Psalm 25:9 NIV

GOD GUIDES

Whether you turn to the right or to the left, your ears will hear a voice behind you, saying, "This is the way; walk in it."

Isaiah 30:21 NIV

Direct my steps by Your word, and let no iniquity have dominion over me.

Psalm 119:133 NKJV

All who are led by the Spirit of God are children of God.

Romans 8:14 NLT

God is our God for ever and ever; He will be our guide even to the end.

Psalm 48:14 NIV

GOD GUIDES

"I will go before you and make the crooked places straight; I will break in pieces the gates of bronze and cut the bars of iron. I will give you the treasures of darkness and hidden riches of secret places, that you may know that I, the LORD, who call you by your name, am the God of Israel."

Isaiah 45:2-3 NKJV

The LORD is good and does what is right; He shows the proper path to those who go astray.

Psalm 25:8 NLT

Thus says the LORD, your Redeemer, the Holy One of Israel: "I am the LORD your God, who teaches you to profit, who leads you in the way you should go."

Isaiah 48:17 ESV

GOD GUIDES

The LORD says, "I will guide you along the best pathway for your life. I will advise you and watch over you. Do not be like a senseless horse or mule that needs a bit and bridle to keep it under control."

Psalm 32:8-9 NLT

May He give you the desire of your heart and make all your plans succeed.

Psalm 20:4 NIV

You will show me the path of life; in Your presence is fullness of joy; at Your right hand are pleasures forevermore.

Psalm 16:11 NKJV

GOD GUIDES

Put your hope in the LORD. Travel steadily along His path.

Psalm 37:34 NLT

The LORD replied, "My Presence will go with you, and I will give you rest."

Exodus 33:14 NIV

All Scripture is breathed out by God and profitable for teaching, for reproof, for correction, and for training in righteousness, that the man of God may be complete, equipped for every good work.

2 Timothy 3:16-17 ESV

Lonely No More

LONELY NO MORE

"Surely I am with you always, to the very end of the age."

Matthew 28:20 NIV

"Whoever does the will of God, he is My brother and sister and mother."

Mark 3:35 ESV

I saw the Lord always before me. Because He is at my right hand, I will not be shaken.

Acts 2:25 NIV

"Your Father already knows your needs."

Luke 12:30 NLT

LONELY NO MORE

"I will be a Father to you, and you will be My sons and daughters, says the Lord Almighty."

2 Corinthians 6:18 NIV

The LORD says, "I will rescue those who love me. I will protect those who trust in My name. When they call on Me, I will answer; I will be with them in trouble. I will rescue and honor them."

Psalm 91:14-15 NLT

O LORD, You have searched me and known me. You know my sitting down and my rising up; You understand my thought afar off. You comprehend my path and my lying down, and are acquainted with all my ways.

Psalm 139:1-3 NKJV

LONELY NO MORE

"No, I will not abandon you as orphans – I will come to you. Soon the world will no longer see Me, but you will see Me. Since I live, you also will live."

John 14:18-19 NLT

"I the LORD your God, will hold your right hand, saying to you, 'Fear not, I will help you.'"

Isaiah 41:13 NKJV

If I go up to the heavens, You are there; if I make my bed in the depths, You are there. If I rise on the wings of the dawn, if I settle on the far side of the sea, even there Your hand will guide me, Your right hand will hold me fast.

Psalm 139:8-10 NIV

LONELY NO MORE

Your righteousness shall go before you; the glory of the LORD shall be your rear guard. Then you shall call, and the LORD will answer; you shall cry, and He will say, "Here I am."

Isaiah 58:8-9 NKJV

"I am with you, and I will protect you wherever you go. One day I will bring you back to this land. I will not leave you until I have finished giving you everything I have promised you."

Genesis 28:15 NLT

Surely the LORD is in this place, and I did not know it.

Genesis 28:16 NKJV

LONELY NO MORE

"If you love Me, obey My commandments. And I will ask the Father, and He will give you another Advocate, who will never leave you. He is the Holy Spirit, who leads into all truth. He lives with you now and later will be in you."

John 14:15-17 NLT

"I will never leave you nor forsake you."

Hebrews 13:5 ESV

The LORD will not forsake His people, for His great name's sake, because it has pleased the LORD to make you His people.

1 Samuel 12:22 NKJV

LONELY NO MORE

One who has unreliable friends soon comes to ruin, but there is a friend who sticks closer than a brother.

Proverbs 18:24 NIV

The LORD will not forsake you nor destroy you, nor forget the covenant of your fathers which He swore to them.

Deuteronomy 4:31 NKJV

The friendship of the LORD is for those who fear Him, and He makes known to them His covenant. My eyes are ever toward the LORD, for He will pluck my feet out of the net. Turn to me and be gracious to me, for I am lonely and afflicted.

Psalm 25:14-16 ESV

LONELY NO MORE

Cast your burden on the LORD, and He shall sustain you; He shall never permit the righteous to be moved.

Psalm 55:22 NKJV

Father to the fatherless, defender of widows – this is God, whose dwelling is holy. God places the lonely in families; He sets the prisoners free and gives them joy.

Psalm 68:5-6 NLT

Though my father and mother forsake me, the LORD will receive me.

Psalm 27:10 NIV

Worry *Less*

WORRY LESS

Cast all your anxiety on Him because He cares for you.

1 Peter 5:7 NIV

Commit everything you do to the LORD. Trust Him, and He will help you.

Psalm 37:5 NLT

"Do not fear, for I am with you; do not be dismayed, for I am your God."

Isaiah 41:10 NIV

The LORD is my light and my salvation; whom shall I fear? The LORD is the strength of my life; of whom shall I be afraid?

Psalm 27:1 NKJV

WORRY LESS

Do not be anxious about anything, but in every situation, by prayer and petition, with thanksgiving, present your requests to God. And the peace of God, which transcends all understanding, will guard your hearts and your minds in Christ Jesus.

Philippians 4:6-7 NIV

Overwhelming victory is ours through Christ, who loved us.

Romans 8:37 NLT

Even though I walk through the valley of the shadow of death, I will fear no evil, for You are with me; Your rod and Your staff, they comfort me.

Psalm 23:4 ESV

WORRY LESS

Jesus said, "Come to Me, all of you who are weary and carry heavy burdens, and I will give you rest. Take My yoke upon you. Let Me teach you, because I am humble and gentle at heart, and you will find rest for your souls. For My yoke is easy to bear, and the burden I give you is light."

Matthew 11:28-30 NLT

I have set the LORD always before me. Because He is at my right hand, I shall not be shaken.

Psalm 16:8 ESV

Do not be afraid and do not panic before them. For the LORD your God will personally go ahead of you. He will neither fail you nor abandon you.

Deuteronomy 31:6 NLT

WORRY LESS

In You, O Lord, I put my trust; let me never be put to shame. Deliver me in Your righteousness, and cause me to escape; incline Your ear to me, and save me.

Psalm 71:1-2 NKJV

In His hand is the life of every creature and the breath of all mankind.

Job 12:10 NIV

Do not be afraid or discouraged, for the Lord will personally go ahead of you. He will be with you; He will neither fail you nor abandon you.

Deuteronomy 31:8 NLT

"Do not be anxious about your life, what you will eat or what you will drink. Look at the birds of the air: they neither sow nor reap nor gather into barns, and yet your heavenly Father feeds them. Are you not of more value than they?"

Matthew 6:25-26 ESV

Be strong, and do not fear, for your God is coming to destroy your enemies. He is coming to save you.

Isaiah 35:4 NLT

"Do not be anxious about how you should defend yourself or what you should say, for the Holy Spirit will teach you in that very hour what you ought to say."

Luke 12:11-12 ESV

WORRY LESS

You will keep in perfect peace all who trust in You, all whose thoughts are fixed on You! Trust in the LORD always, for the LORD GOD is the eternal Rock.

Isaiah 26:3-4 NLT

"Be still, and know that I am God."

Psalm 46:10 ESV

"Fear not, for I have redeemed you; I have called you by your name; you are Mine."

Isaiah 43:1 NKJV

When I am afraid, I will put my trust in You.

Psalm 56:3 NLT

WORRY LESS

"Do not be anxious about tomorrow, for tomorrow will be anxious for itself. Sufficient for the day is its own trouble."

Matthew 6:34 ESV

Anxiety weighs down the heart, but a kind word cheers it up.

Proverbs 12:25 NIV

"Look at the ravens. They don't plant or harvest or store food in barns, for God feeds them. And you are far more valuable to Him than any birds!"

Luke 12:24 NLT

When in *Doubt*

WHEN IN DOUBT

"As the lightning flashes and lights up the sky from one end to the other, so it will be on the day when the Son of Man comes."

Luke 17:24 NLT

Lord, I believe; help my unbelief!

Mark 9:24 NKJV

"Stop doubting and believe."

John 20:27 NIV

God has not given us a spirit of fear, but of power and of love and of a sound mind.

2 Timothy 1:7 NKJV

WHEN IN DOUBT

Jesus immediately reached out His hand and took hold of him, saying, "O you of little faith, why did you doubt?"

Matthew 14:31 ESV

It is impossible to please God without faith. Anyone who wants to come to Him must believe that God exists and that He rewards those who sincerely seek Him.

Hebrews 11:6 NLT

Look, I go forward, but He is not there, and backward, but I cannot perceive Him; when He works on the left hand, I cannot behold Him; when He turns to the right hand, I cannot see Him. But He knows the way that I take; when He has tested me, I shall come forth as gold.

Job 23:8-10 NKJV

WHEN IN DOUBT

If any of you lacks wisdom, let him ask God, who gives generously to all without reproach, and it will be given him. But let him ask in faith, with no doubting.

James 1:5-6 ESV

Build each other up in your most holy faith … And show mercy to those whose faith is wavering.

Jude 20, 22 NLT

Jesus said to them, "Why are you troubled? And why do doubts arise in your hearts? Behold My hands and My feet, that it is I Myself."

Luke 24:38-39 NKJV

WHEN IN DOUBT

When doubts filled my mind, Your comfort gave me renewed hope and cheer.

Psalm 94:19 NLT

"'My purpose will stand, and I will do all that I please.' What I have said, that I will bring about; what I have planned, that I will do."

Isaiah 46:10-11 NIV

"Have faith in God. I tell you the truth, you can say to this mountain, 'May you be lifted up and thrown into the sea,' and it will happen. But you must really believe it will happen and have no doubt in your heart."

Mark 11:22-23 NLT

The Lord is not slow to fulfill His promise as some count slowness, but is patient toward you, not wishing that any should perish, but that all should reach repentance.

2 Peter 3:9 ESV

God's way is perfect. All the LORD's promises prove true. He is a shield for all who look to Him for protection.

Psalm 18:30 NLT

Jesus said to him, "'If you can'! All things are possible for one who believes."

Mark 9:23 ESV

WHEN IN DOUBT

Listen! The LORD's arm is not too weak to save you, nor is His ear too deaf to hear you call.

Isaiah 59:1 NLT

Trust in the LORD with all your heart, and lean not on your own understanding; in all your ways acknowledge Him, and He shall direct your paths.

Proverbs 3:5-7 NKJV

Jesus replied, "Truly I tell you, if you have faith and do not doubt, not only can you do what was done to the fig tree, but also you can say to this mountain, 'Go, throw yourself into the sea,' and it will be done."

Matthew 21:21 NIV

WHEN IN DOUBT

"Call upon Me in the day of trouble; I will deliver you, and you shall glorify Me."

Psalm 50:15 NKJV

Then Jesus told him, "You believe because you have seen Me. Blessed are those who believe without seeing Me."

John 20:29 NLT

He said to them, "Why are you afraid, O you of little faith?" Then He rose and rebuked the winds and the sea, and there was a great calm.

Matthew 8:26 ESV

Times of Trial

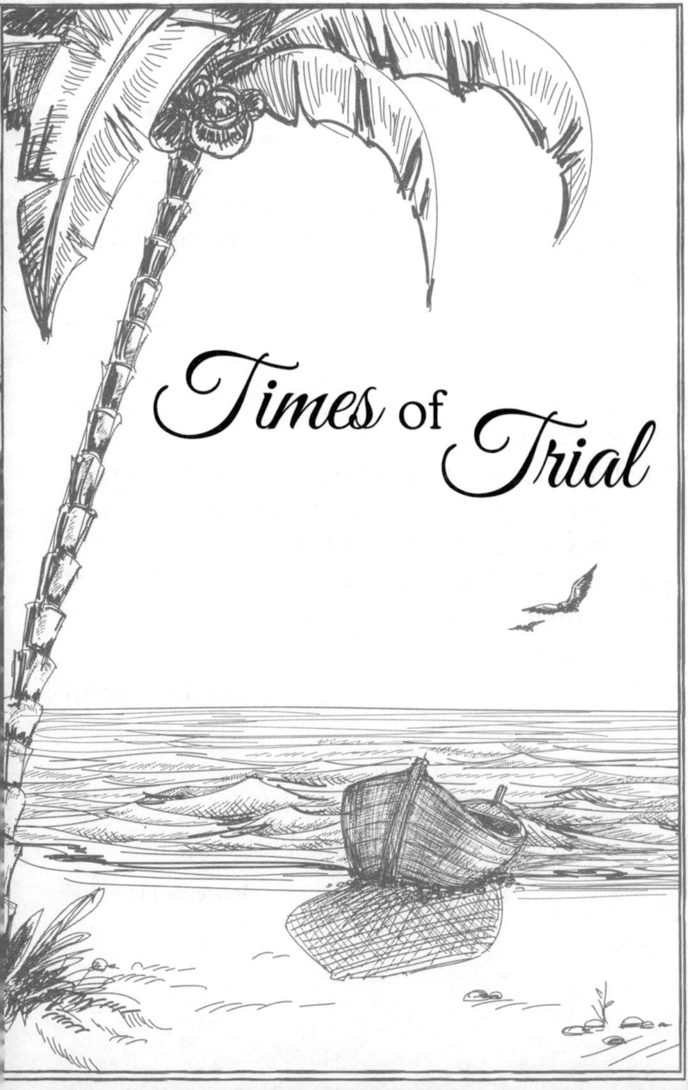

TIMES OF TRIAL

I consider that the sufferings of this present time are not worth comparing with the glory that is to be revealed to us.

Romans 8:18 ESV

Beloved, do not think it strange concerning the fiery trial which is to try you, as though some strange thing happened to you; but rejoice to the extent that you partake of Christ's sufferings, that when His glory is revealed, you may also be glad with exceeding joy.

1 Peter 4:12-13 NKJV

God had planned something better for us.

Hebrews 11:40 NIV

TIMES OF TRIAL

Through Him we have also obtained access by faith into this grace in which we stand, and we rejoice in hope of the glory of God. Not only that, but we rejoice in our sufferings, knowing that suffering produces endurance, and endurance produces character, and character produces hope, and hope does not put us to shame, because God's love has been poured into our hearts through the Holy Spirit who has been given to us.

Romans 5:2-5 ESV

Consider it pure joy, my brothers and sisters, whenever you face trials of many kinds, because you know that the testing of your faith develops perseverance. Let perseverance finish its work so that you may be mature and complete, not lacking anything.

James 1:2-4 NIV

Since He Himself has gone through suffering and testing, He is able to help us when we are being tested.

Hebrews 2:18 NLT

The God of all grace, who called you to His eternal glory in Christ, after you have suffered a little while, will Himself restore you and make you strong, firm and steadfast.

1 Peter 5:10 NIV

As the elect of God, holy and beloved, put on tender mercies, kindness, humility, meekness, longsuffering.

Colossians 3:12 NKJV

TIMES OF TRIAL

"In Me you may have peace. In this world you will have trouble. But take heart! I have overcome the world."

John 16:33 NIV

The more we suffer for Christ, the more God will shower us with His comfort through Christ.

2 Corinthians 1:5 NLT

Those who suffer according to God's will should commit themselves to their faithful Creator and continue to do good.

1 Peter 4:19 NIV

"When you go through deep waters, I will be with you. When you go through rivers of difficulty, you will not drown. When you walk through the fire of oppression, you will not be burned up; the flames will not consume you."

Isaiah 43:2 NLT

If you suffer for doing good and you endure it, this is commendable before God. To this you were called, because Christ suffered for you, leaving you an example, that you should follow in His steps.

1 Peter 2:20-21 NIV

What then shall we say to these things? If God is for us, who can be against us?

Romans 8:31 ESV

TIMES OF TRIAL

Blessed is the one who perseveres under trial because, having stood the test, that person will receive the crown of life that the Lord has promised to those who love Him.

James 1:12 NIV

I love the LORD because He hears my voice and my prayer for mercy. Because He bends down to listen, I will pray as long as I have breath!

Psalm 116:1-2 NLT

Be strong and do not give up, for your work will be rewarded.

2 Chronicles 15:7 NIV

The Lord knows how to rescue godly people from their trials.

2 Peter 2:9 NLT

Let us throw off everything that hinders and the sin that so easily entangles. And let us run with perseverance the race marked out for us.

Hebrews 12:1 NIV

"Don't let your hearts be troubled. Trust in God, and trust also in Me."

John 14:1 NLT

The Lord sustains them on their sickbed and restores them from their bed of illness.

Psalm 41:3 NIV

Talk to the Lord

Confess your sins to each other and pray for each other so that you may be healed. The prayer of a righteous person is powerful and effective.

James 5:16 NIV

Devote yourselves to prayer with an alert mind and a thankful heart.

Colossians 4:2 NLT

Pray in the Spirit on all occasions with all kinds of prayers and requests. With this in mind, be alert and always keep on praying for all the Lord's people.

Ephesians 6:18 NIV

TALK TO THE LORD

LORD, I cry out to You; make haste to me! Give ear to my voice when I cry out to You. Let my prayer be set before You as incense, the lifting up of my hands as the evening sacrifice.

Psalm 141:1-2 NKJV

"When you pray, go into your room, close the door and pray to your Father, who is unseen. Then your Father, who sees what is done in secret, will reward you."

Matthew 6:6 NIV

The LORD delights in the prayers of the upright.

Proverbs 15:8 NLT

TALK TO THE LORD

Rejoice always, pray continually, give thanks in all circumstances; for this is God's will for you in Christ Jesus.

1 Thessalonians 5:16-18 NIV

"When you pray, do not use vain repetitions as the heathen do. For they think that they will be heard for their many words. Therefore do not be like them. For your Father knows the things you have need of before you ask Him."

Matthew 6:7-8 NKJV

"Watch and pray so that you will not fall into temptation. The spirit is willing, but the flesh is weak."

Matthew 26:41 NIV

TALK TO THE LORD

Is anyone among you in trouble? Let them pray. Is anyone happy? Let them sing songs of praise. Is anyone among you sick? Let them call the elders of the church to pray over them and anoint them with oil in the name of the Lord.

James 5:13-14 NIV

I confessed all my sins to You and stopped trying to hide my guilt. I said to myself, "I will confess my rebellion to the LORD." And You forgave me! All my guilt is gone. Therefore, let all the godly pray to You while there is still time, that they may not drown in the floodwaters of judgment.

Psalm 32:5-6 NLT

"If you believe, you will receive whatever you ask for in prayer."

Matthew 21:22 NIV

TALK TO THE LORD

This is the confidence that we have in Him, that if we ask anything according to His will, He hears us. And if we know that He hears us, whatever we ask, we know that we have the petitions that we have asked of Him.

1 John 5:14-15 NKJV

The eyes of the Lord are on the righteous and His ears are attentive to their prayer.

1 Peter 3:12 NIV

"I tell you, you can pray for anything, and if you believe that you've received it, it will be yours."

Mark 11:24 NLT

TALK TO THE LORD

Truly God has listened; He has attended to the voice of my prayer. Blessed be God, because He has not rejected my prayer or removed His steadfast love from me!

Psalm 66:19-20 ESV

"If My people who are called by My name will humble themselves, and pray and seek My face, and turn from their wicked ways, then I will hear from heaven, and will forgive their sin and heal their land."

2 Chronicles 7:14 NKJV

The LORD hears His people when they call to Him for help. He rescues them from all their troubles.

Psalm 34:17 NLT

In my distress I called upon the LORD, and cried out to my God; He heard my voice from His temple, and my cry came before Him, even to His ears.

Psalm 18:6 NKJV

They cried to the LORD in their trouble, and He delivered them from their distress.

Psalm 107:28 ESV

"If you remain in Me and My words remain in you, ask whatever you wish, and it will be done for you."

John 15:7 NIV

Continually *Seek Him*

CONTINUALLY SEEK HIM

Let the hearts of those who seek the LORD rejoice! Seek the LORD and His strength; seek His presence continually! Remember the wondrous works that He has done, His miracles and the judgments He uttered. He is the LORD our God; His judgments are in all the earth.

1 Chronicles 16:10-12, 14 ESV

I seek You with all my heart; do not let me stray from Your commands.

Psalm 119:10 NIV

Let all those who seek You rejoice and be glad in You; let such as love Your salvation say continually, "The LORD be magnified!"

Psalm 40:16 NKJV

CONTINUALLY SEEK HIM

Draw near to God, and He will draw near to you.

James 4:8 ESV

Those who know Your name will put their trust in You; for You, LORD, have not forsaken those who seek You. Sing praises to the LORD, who dwells in Zion! Declare His deeds among the people.

Psalm 9:10-11 NKJV

My heart says of You, "Seek His face!" Your face, LORD, I will seek. Do not hide Your face from me, do not turn Your servant away in anger; You have been my helper.

Psalm 27:8-9 NIV

CONTINUALLY SEEK HIM

Seek the LORD your God, and you will find Him if you seek Him with all your heart and with all your soul.

Deuteronomy 4:29 NKJV

"Ask, and it will be given to you; seek, and you will find; knock, and it will be opened to you. For everyone who asks receives, and the one who seeks finds, and to the one who knocks it will be opened."

Matthew 7:7-8 ESV

I love those who love me, and those who seek me diligently will find me.

Proverbs 8:17 NKJV

CONTINUALLY SEEK HIM

"Whoever believes in Me, as Scripture has said, rivers of living water will flow from within them." By this He meant the Spirit, whom those who believed in Him were later to receive.

John 7:38-39 NIV

Glory in His holy name; let the hearts of those rejoice who seek the LORD! Seek the LORD and His strength; seek His face evermore!

Psalm 105:3-4 NKJV

The LORD looks down from heaven on all mankind to see if there are any who understand, any who seek God.

Psalm 14:2 NIV

CONTINUALLY SEEK HIM

The LORD is with you while you are with Him. If you seek Him, He will be found by you, but if you forsake Him, He will forsake you.

2 Chronicles 15:2 ESV

The lions may grow weak and hungry, but those who seek the LORD lack no good thing.

Psalm 34:10 NIV

He made from one man every nation of mankind to live on all the face of the earth, having determined allotted periods and the boundaries of their dwelling place, that they should seek God, and perhaps feel their way toward Him and find Him. Yet He is actually not far from each one of us.

Acts 17:26-27 ESV

CONTINUALLY SEEK HIM

Devote your heart and soul to seeking the LORD your God.

1 Chronicles 22:19 NIV

"Your heavenly Father already knows all your needs. Seek the Kingdom of God above all else, and live righteously, and He will give you everything you need."

Matthew 6:32-33 NLT

If then you were raised with Christ, seek those things which are above, where Christ is, sitting at the right hand of God. Set your mind on things above, not on things on the earth.

Colossians 3:1-2 NKJV

CONTINUALLY SEEK HIM

You, God, are my God, earnestly I seek You;
I thirst for You, my whole being longs for You,
in a dry and parched land where there is no water.

Psalm 63:1 NIV

Seek the LORD while He may be found; call upon Him while He is near.

Isaiah 55:6 ESV

The LORD sees every heart and knows every plan and thought. If you seek Him, you will find Him. But if you forsake Him, He will reject you forever.

1 Chronicles 28:9 NLT

An *Omnipresent God*

AN OMNIPRESENT GOD

"The kingdom of God is within you."

Luke 17:21 NKJV

Be strong and courageous. The LORD your God will be with you wherever you go.

Joshua 1:9 NIV

"Where two or three are gathered together in My name, I am there in the midst of them."

Matthew 18:20 NKJV

Let us hold fast the confession of our hope without wavering, for He who promised is faithful.

Hebrews 10:23 ESV

AN OMNIPRESENT GOD

Because of Christ and our faith in Him, we can now come boldly and confidently into God's presence.

Ephesians 3:12 NLT

"Anyone who loves Me will obey My teaching. My Father will love them, and We will come to them and make Our home with them. Anyone who does not love Me will not obey My teaching."

John 14:23-24 NIV

Surely Your goodness and unfailing love will pursue me all the days of my life, and I will live in the house of the LORD forever.

Psalm 23:6 NLT

AN OMNIPRESENT GOD

The LORD your God is with you, the Mighty Warrior who saves. He will take great delight in you; in His love He will no longer rebuke you, but will rejoice over you with singing.

Zephaniah 3:17 NIV

There is one Lord, one faith, one baptism, one God and Father of all, who is over all, in all, and living through all.

Ephesians 4:5-6 NLT

The eyes of the LORD are in every place, keeping watch on the evil and the good.

Proverbs 15:3 NKJV

AN OMNIPRESENT GOD

"I will be your God throughout your lifetime – until your hair is white with age. I made you and I will care for you. I will carry you along and save you."

Isaiah 46:4 NLT

He is before all things, and in Him all things hold together. And He is the head of the body, the church. He is the beginning, the firstborn from the dead, that in everything He might be preeminent.

Colossians 1:17-18 ESV

"If you look for Me wholeheartedly, you will find Me."

Jeremiah 29:13 NLT

AN OMNIPRESENT GOD

"Where were you when I laid the foundations of the earth? Tell Me, if you have understanding. Who determined its measurements? Surely you know! Or who stretched the line upon it? To what were its foundations fastened? Or who laid its cornerstone, when the morning stars sang together, and all the sons of God shouted for joy?"

Job 38:4-7 NKJV

God watches how people live; He sees everything they do.

Job 34:21 NLT

In peace I will lie down and sleep, for You alone, LORD, make me dwell in safety.

Psalm 4:8 NIV

AN OMNIPRESENT GOD

Can you solve the mysteries of God? Can you discover everything about the Almighty? Such knowledge is higher than the heavens – and who are you? It is deeper than the underworld – what do you know? It is broader than the earth and wider than the sea.

Job 11:7-9 NLT

The word of God is alive and active. Sharper than any double-edged sword, it penetrates even to dividing soul and spirit, joints and marrow; it judges the thoughts and attitudes of the heart. Nothing in all creation is hidden from God's sight. Everything is uncovered and laid bare before the eyes of Him to whom we must give account.

Hebrews 4:12-13 NIV

AN OMNIPRESENT GOD

"Can anyone hide from Me in a secret place? Am I not everywhere in all the heavens and earth?" says the LORD.

Jeremiah 23:24 NLT

For this is what the high and exalted One says – He who lives forever, whose name is holy: "I live in a high and holy place, but also with the one who is contrite and lowly in spirit, to revive the spirit of the lowly and to revive the heart of the contrite."

Isaiah 57:15 NIV

God is with those who obey Him.

Psalm 14:5 NLT

Unfailing *Love*

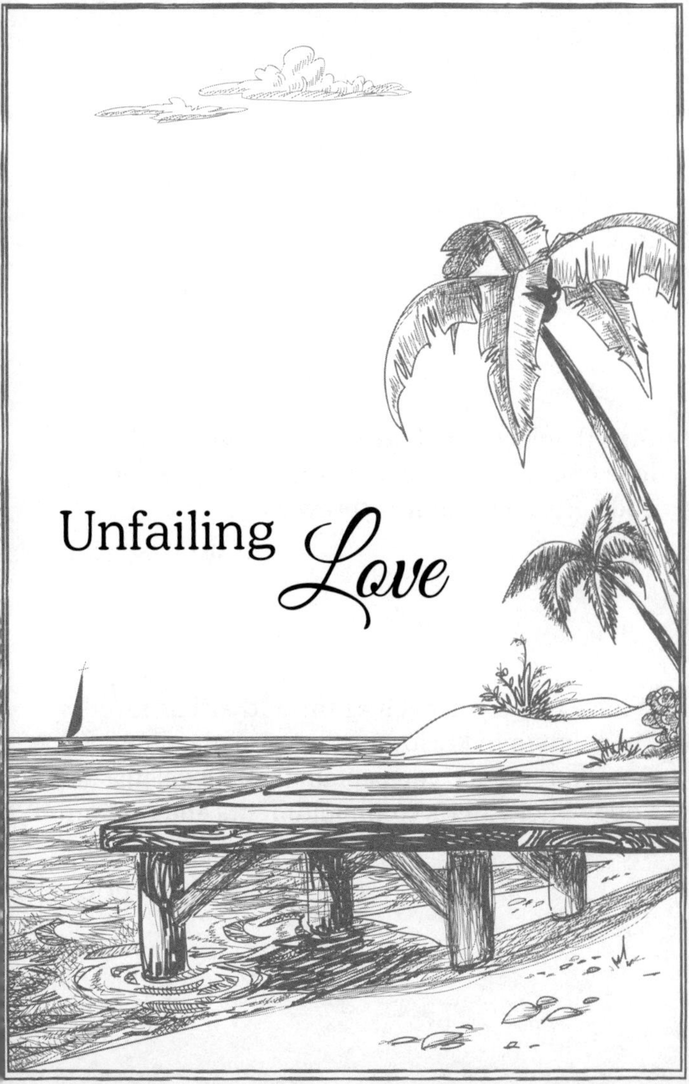

UNFAILING LOVE

"The Son of Man came to seek and to save the lost."

Luke 19:10 ESV

Give thanks to the LORD, for He is good. His love endures forever. Give thanks to the God of gods. His love endures forever.

Psalm 136:1-2 NIV

"I have loved you even as the Father has loved Me. Remain in My love. When you obey My commandments, you remain in My love, just as I obey My Father's commandments and remain in His love."

John 15:9-10 NLT

See how very much our Father loves us, for He calls us His children, and that is what we are!

1 John 3:1 NLT

Neither death nor life, neither angels nor demons, neither the present nor the future, nor any powers, neither height nor depth, nor anything else in all creation, will be able to separate us from the love of God.

Romans 8:38-39 NIV

No temptation has overtaken you except such as is common to man; but God is faithful, who will not allow you to be tempted beyond what you are able, but with the temptation will also make the way of escape, that you may be able to bear it.

1 Corinthians 10:13 NKJV

"I am the good shepherd. The good shepherd lays down His life for the sheep."

John 10:11 NIV

"I lavish unfailing love for a thousand generations to those who love Me and obey My commands."

Deuteronomy 5:10 NLT

Enter into His gates with thanksgiving, and into His courts with praise. Be thankful to Him, and bless His name. For the LORD is good; His mercy is everlasting, and His truth endures to all generations.

Psalm 100:4-5 NKJV

UNFAILING LOVE

This is how God showed His love among us: He sent His one and only Son into the world that we might live through Him. This is love: not that we loved God, but that He loved us and sent His Son as an atoning sacrifice for our sins.

1 John 4:9-10 NIV

The faithful love of the LORD never ends! His mercies never cease. Great is His faithfulness; His mercies begin afresh each morning.

Lamentations 3:22-23 NLT

"For God so loved the world that He gave His one and only Son, that whoever believes in Him shall not perish but have eternal life."

John 3:16 NIV

UNFAILING LOVE

Your unfailing love, O LORD, is as vast as the heavens; Your faithfulness reaches beyond the clouds. Your righteousness is like the mighty mountains, Your justice like the ocean depths. You care for people and animals alike, O LORD.

Psalm 36:5-6 NLT

"I have loved you with an everlasting love; I have drawn you with unfailing kindness."

Jeremiah 31:3 NIV

Praise the LORD, all nations! Extol Him, all peoples! For great is His steadfast love toward us, and the faithfulness of the LORD endures forever. Praise the LORD!

Psalm 117:1-2 ESV

UNFAILING LOVE

I will sing of the LORD's great love forever. I will declare that Your love stands firm forever, that You have established Your faithfulness in heaven itself.

Psalm 89:1-2 NIV

It is good to give thanks to the LORD, to sing praises to Your name, O Most High; to declare Your steadfast love in the morning, and Your faithfulness by night, to the music of the lute and the harp, to the melody of the lyre.

Psalm 92:1-3 ESV

Give thanks to the LORD, for He is good! His faithful love endures forever.

Psalm 106:1 NLT

UNFAILING LOVE

He will love you and bless you.

Deuteronomy 7:13 NKJV

"Greater love has no one than this: to lay down one's life for one's friends."

John 15:13 NIV

Let us love one another, for love is from God, and whoever loves has been born of God and knows God. Anyone who does not love does not know God, because God is love.

1 John 4:7-8 ESV

Find *Shelter* in God

FIND SHELTER IN GOD

He who dwells in the shelter of the Most High will rest in the shadow of the Almighty.

Psalm 91:1 NIV

Let all who take refuge in You rejoice; let them sing joyful praises forever. Spread Your protection over them, that all who love Your name may be filled with joy. For You bless the godly, O LORD; You surround them with Your shield of love.

Psalm 5:11-12 NLT

The eternal God is your refuge, and underneath are the everlasting arms.

Deuteronomy 33:27 NIV

FIND SHELTER IN GOD

He will deliver you from the snare of the fowler and from the deadly pestilence. He will cover you with His pinions, and under His wings you will find refuge.

Psalm 91:3-4 ESV

The LORD is my rock, my fortress and my deliverer; my God is my rock, in whom I take refuge.

Psalm 18:2 NIV

You have been a shelter for me, a strong tower from the enemy. I will abide in Your tabernacle forever; I will trust in the shelter of Your wings.

Psalm 61:3-4 NKJV

FIND SHELTER IN GOD

I will say of the LORD, "He is my refuge and my fortress, my God, in whom I trust."

Psalm 91:2 NIV

The LORD redeems the life of His servants; none of those who take refuge in Him will be condemned.

Psalm 34:22 ESV

The LORD is good, a refuge in times of trouble. He cares for those who trust in Him.

Nahum 1:7 NIV

Trust in Him at all times. Pour out your heart to Him, for God is our refuge.

Psalm 62:8 NLT

FIND SHELTER IN GOD

Every word of God proves true; He is a shield to those who take refuge in Him.

Proverbs 30:5 ESV

Those who fear the LORD are secure; He will be a refuge for their children.

Proverbs 14:26 NLT

For in the day of trouble He will keep me safe in His dwelling; He will hide me in the shelter of His sacred tent and set me high upon a rock. Then my head will be exalted above the enemies who surround me; at His sacred tent I will sacrifice with shouts of joy; I will sing and make music to the LORD.

Psalm 27:5-6 NIV

FIND SHELTER IN GOD

You have been a strength to the poor, a strength to the needy in his distress, a refuge from the storm, a shade from the heat; for the blast of the terrible ones is as a storm against the wall.

Isaiah 25:4 NKJV

You are my refuge and my shield; I have put my hope in Your word.

Psalm 119:114 NIV

Be my rock of safety where I can always hide. Give the order to save me, for You are my rock and my fortress. My God, rescue me from the power of the wicked, from the clutches of cruel oppressors.

Psalm 71:3-4 NLT

FIND SHELTER IN GOD

The name of the LORD is a strong tower;
the righteous man runs into it and is safe.

Proverbs 18:10 ESV

Have mercy on me, O God, have mercy! I look to You for protection. I will hide beneath the shadow of Your wings until the danger passes by. I cry out to God Most High, to God who will fulfill His purpose for me. He will send help from heaven to rescue me, disgracing those who hound me. My God will send forth His unfailing love and faithfulness.

Psalm 57:1-3 NLT

You are my hiding place; You shall preserve me from trouble; You shall surround me with songs of deliverance.

Psalm 32:7 NKJV

FIND SHELTER IN GOD

My God is my rock, in whom I find protection. He is my shield, the power that saves me, and my place of safety. He is my refuge, my savior, the one who saves me from violence.

2 Samuel 22:3 NLT

I will sing of Your strength, in the morning I will sing of Your love; for You are my fortress, my refuge in times of trouble.

Psalm 59:16 NIV

The LORD is a shelter for the oppressed, a refuge in times of trouble.

Psalm 9:9 NLT

Strength in the Lord

STRENGTH IN THE LORD

The joy of the LORD is your strength!

Nehemiah 8:10 NLT

Be strong in the Lord and in His mighty power. Put on the full armor of God, so that you can take your stand against the devil's schemes.

Ephesians 6:10-11 NIV

God is our refuge and strength, an ever-present help in trouble. Therefore we will not fear, though the earth give way and the mountains fall into the heart of the sea, though its waters roar and foam and the mountains quake with their surging.

Psalm 46:1-3 NIV

STRENGTH IN THE LORD

May our Lord Jesus Christ, who loved us, strengthen you in every good thing you do and say.

2 Thessalonians 2:16-17 NLT

The LORD sits enthroned over the flood; the LORD is enthroned as King forever. The LORD gives strength to His people; the LORD blesses His people with peace.

Psalm 29:10-11 NIV

This is what the Sovereign LORD, the Holy One of Israel, says: "In repentance and rest is your salvation, in quietness and trust is your strength."

Isaiah 30:15 NIV

Turn to God. Then times of refreshment will come from the presence of the Lord, and He will again send you Jesus, your appointed Messiah.

Acts 3:19-20 NLT

The Sovereign LORD is my strength; He makes my feet like the feet of a deer, He enables me to go on the heights.

Habakkuk 3:19 NIV

He said to Me, "My grace is sufficient for you, for My strength is made perfect in weakness." Therefore most gladly I will rather boast in my infirmities, that the power of Christ may rest upon me.

2 Corinthians 12:9 NKJV

"I will search for My lost ones, and I will bring them safely home again. I will bandage the injured and strengthen the weak."

Ezekiel 34:16 NLT

God is my strength and power, and He makes my way perfect. He makes my feet like the feet of deer, and sets me on my high places. He teaches my hands to make war, so that my arms can bend a bow of bronze.

2 Samuel 22:33-35 NKJV

Ah, Lord GOD! It is You who have made the heavens and the earth by Your great power and by Your outstretched arm! Nothing is too hard for You.

Jeremiah 32:17 ESV

I thank and praise You, God of my ancestors, for You have given me wisdom and strength.

Daniel 2:23 NLT

Honor and majesty are before Him; strength and gladness are in His place.

1 Chronicles 16:27 NKJV

My health may fail, and my spirit may grow weak, but God remains the strength of my heart; He is mine forever. How good it is to be near God! I have made the Sovereign LORD my shelter, and I will tell everyone about the wonderful things You do.

Psalm 73:26, 28 NLT

STRENGTH IN THE LORD

The LORD is my strength and my song; He has given me victory.

Psalm 118:14 NLT

Now to Him who is able to do immeasurably more than all we ask or imagine, according to His power that is at work within us, to Him be glory in the church and in Christ Jesus throughout all generations, for ever and ever!

Ephesians 3:20-21 NIV

Yours, O LORD, is the greatness, the power and the glory, the victory and the majesty; for all that is in heaven and in earth is Yours; Yours is the kingdom, O LORD, and You are exalted as head over all.

1 Chronicles 29:11 NKJV

I can do all things through Christ who strengthens me.

Philippians 4:13 NKJV

In Your strength I can crush an army; with my God I can scale any wall.

Psalm 18:29 NLT

He gives strength to the weary and increases the power of the weak.

Isaiah 40:29 NIV

The LORD is my strength and my defense; He has become my salvation.

Exodus 15:2 NIV

God Is Our *Helper*

GOD IS OUR HELPER

I will lift up my eyes to the hills – from whence comes my help? My help comes from the LORD, who made heaven and earth.

Psalm 121:1-2 NKJV

The LORD is my strength and my shield; in Him my heart trusts, and I am helped; my heart exults, and with my song I give thanks to Him. The LORD is the strength of His people; He is the saving refuge of His anointed.

Psalm 28:7-8 ESV

Our help is from the LORD, who made heaven and earth.

Psalm 124:8 NLT

GOD IS OUR HELPER

Those who look to Him for help will be radiant with joy; no shadow of shame will darken their faces.

Psalm 34:5 NLT

We may boldly say: "The Lord is my helper;
I will not fear. What can man do to me?"

Hebrews 13:6 NKJV

Joyful are those who have the God of Israel as their helper, whose hope is in the LORD their God. He made heaven and earth, the sea, and everything in them. He keeps every promise forever.

Psalm 146:5-6 NLT

GOD IS OUR HELPER

The Spirit also helps in our weaknesses. For we do not know what we should pray for as we ought, but the Spirit Himself makes intercession for us with groanings which cannot be uttered.

Romans 8:26 NKJV

I will be fully satisfied as with the richest of foods; with singing lips my mouth will praise You. Because You are my help, I sing in the shadow of Your wings.

Psalm 63:5, 7 NIV

You are from God and have overcome them, for He who is in you is greater than he who is in the world.

1 John 4:4 ESV

GOD IS OUR HELPER

Surely God is my help; the Lord is the one who sustains me.

Psalm 54:4 NIV

The LORD is for me; He will help me. I will look in triumph at those who hate me. It is better to take refuge in the LORD than to trust in people.

Psalm 118:7-8 NLT

All kings shall fall down before Him; all nations shall serve Him. For He will deliver the needy when he cries, the poor also, and him who has no helper.

Psalm 72:11-12 NKJV

GOD IS OUR HELPER

As for me, I am poor and needy; may the Lord think of me. You are my help and my deliverer; You are my God, do not delay.

Psalm 40:17 NIV

"It is to your advantage that I go away, for if I do not go away, the Helper will not come to you. But if I go, I will send Him to you."

John 16:7 ESV

"The Helper, the Holy Spirit, whom the Father will send in My name, He will teach you all things, and bring to your remembrance all things that I said to you."

John 14:26 NKJV

GOD IS OUR HELPER

The righteous person faces many troubles,
but the LORD comes to the rescue each time.
The LORD protects the bones of the righteous;
not one of them is broken!

Psalm 34:19-20 NLT

I will praise Your name, LORD, for it is good.
You have delivered me from all my troubles,
and my eyes have looked in triumph on my foes.

Psalm 54:6-7 NIV

The LORD rescues the godly; He is their fortress in times of trouble. The LORD helps them, rescuing them from the wicked.

Psalm 37:39-40 NLT

GOD IS OUR HELPER

The LORD will fight for you, and you have only to be silent.

Exodus 14:14 ESV

In my desperation I prayed, and the LORD listened; He saved me from all my troubles. For the angel of the LORD is a guard; He surrounds and defends all who fear Him. Taste and see that the LORD is good. Oh, the joys of those who take refuge in Him!

Psalm 34:6-8 NLT

Our soul waits for the LORD; He is our help and our shield. For our heart shall rejoice in Him, because we have trusted in His holy name.

Psalm 33:20-21 NKJV

God's Comfort

"Do not be afraid, for I am with you; I will bless you."

Genesis 26:24 NIV

You give them relief from troubled times. The LORD will not reject His people; He will not abandon His special possession.

Psalm 94:13-14 NLT

How good it is to sing praises to our God, how pleasant and fitting to praise Him! He heals the brokenhearted and binds up their wounds. He determines the number of the stars and calls them each by name.

Psalm 147:1, 3-4 NIV

GOD'S COMFORT

"Blessed are those who mourn, for they will be comforted."

Matthew 5:4 NIV

"I, yes I, am the one who comforts you. So why are you afraid?"

Isaiah 51:12 NLT

Though You have made me see troubles, many and bitter, You will restore my life again; from the depths of the earth You will again bring me up. You will increase my honor and comfort me once more.

Psalm 71:20-21 NIV

Though I walk in the midst of trouble, You preserve my life; You stretch out Your hand against the wrath of my enemies, and Your right hand delivers me.

Psalm 138:7 ESV

As the deer longs for streams of water, so I long for You, O God. I thirst for God, the living God. When can I go and stand before Him?

Psalm 42:1-2 NLT

The LORD upholds all who fall, and raises up all who are bowed down.

Psalm 145:14 NKJV

GOD'S COMFORT

Come, let us bow down in worship, let us kneel before the LORD our Maker; for He is our God and we are the people of His pasture, the flock under His care.

Psalm 95:6-7 NIV

The LORD is close to the brokenhearted; He rescues those whose spirits are crushed.

Psalm 34:18 NLT

"Can a mother forget the baby at her breast and have no compassion on the child she has borne? Though she may forget, I will not forget you! See, I have engraved you on the palms of My hands; your walls are ever before Me."

Isaiah 49:15-16 NIV

GOD'S COMFORT

Weeping may endure for a night, but joy comes in the morning.

Psalm 30:5 NKJV

Praise be to the God and Father of our Lord Jesus Christ, the Father of compassion and the God of all comfort, who comforts us in all our troubles.

2 Corinthians 1:3-4 NIV

Aim for restoration, comfort one another, agree with one another, live in peace; and the God of love and peace will be with you.

2 Corinthians 13:11 ESV

GOD'S COMFORT

"As a mother comforts her child, so will I comfort you."

Isaiah 66:13 NIV

How great is the goodness you have stored up for those who fear You. You lavish it on those who come to You for protection, blessing them before the watching world.

Psalm 31:19 NLT

Shout for joy, you heavens; rejoice, you earth; burst into song, you mountains! For the LORD comforts His people and will have compassion on His afflicted ones.

Isaiah 49:13 NIV

GOD'S COMFORT

Let Your unfailing love comfort me, just as You promised me.

Psalm 119:76 NLT

We know that in all things God works for the good of those who love Him.

Romans 8:28 NIV

This is my comfort in my affliction, that Your promise gives me life.

Psalm 119:50 ESV

Give me a sign of Your goodness, that my enemies may see it and be put to shame, for You, LORD, have helped me and comforted me.

Psalm 86:17 NIV

Trust in the Lord

TRUST IN THE LORD

Put your trust in the LORD.

Psalm 4:5 NKJV

Many will see and fear, and put their trust in the LORD. Blessed is the man who makes the LORD his trust, who does not turn to the proud, to those who go astray after a lie! You have multiplied, O LORD my God, Your wondrous deeds and Your thoughts toward us; none can compare with You!

Psalm 40:3-5 ESV

When I am in distress, I call to You, because You answer me.

Psalm 86:7 NIV

TRUST IN THE LORD

I pray that God, the source of hope, will fill you completely with joy and peace because you trust in Him. Then you will overflow with confident hope through the power of the Holy Spirit.

Romans 15:13 NLT

Submit to God and be at peace with Him; in this way prosperity will come to you.

Job 22:21 NIV

Let me hear of Your unfailing love each morning, for I am trusting You. Show me where to walk, for I give myself to You. Rescue me from my enemies, LORD; I run to You to hide me.

Psalm 143:8-9 NLT

TRUST IN THE LORD

Blessed is the one who trusts in the LORD, whose confidence is in Him. They will be like a tree planted by the water that sends out its roots by the stream. It does not fear when heat comes; its leaves are always green. It has no worries in a year of drought and never fails to bear fruit.

Jeremiah 17:7-8 NIV

The fear of man brings a snare, but whoever trusts in the LORD shall be safe.

Proverbs 29:25 NKJV

Faith is confidence in what we hope for and assurance about what we do not see.

Hebrews 11:1 NIV

TRUST IN THE LORD

We don't look at the troubles we can see now; rather, we fix our gaze on things that cannot be seen. For the things we see now will soon be gone, but the things we cannot see will last forever.

2 Corinthians 4:18 NLT

Be on your guard; stand firm in the faith; be courageous; be strong.

1 Corinthians 16:13 NIV

The LORD is righteous in all His ways and faithful in all He does. The LORD is near to all who call on Him, to all who call on Him in truth.

Psalm 145:17-18 NIV

It is by grace you have been saved, through faith – and this not from yourselves, it is the gift of God.

Ephesians 2:8 NIV

As the Scriptures tell us, "Anyone who trusts in Him will never be disgraced."

Romans 10:11 NLT

Since we have been justified through faith, we have peace with God through our Lord Jesus Christ, through whom we have gained access by faith into this grace in which we now stand.

Romans 5:1-2 NIV

I praise God for what He has promised. I trust in God, so why should I be afraid? What can mere mortals do to me?

Psalm 56:4 NLT

May the LORD answer you when you are in distress; may the name of the God of Jacob protect you.

Psalm 20:1 NIV

Let not steadfast love and faithfulness forsake you; bind them around your neck; write them on the tablet of your heart.

Proverbs 3:3 ESV